PIANO • VOCAL • GUITAR

THE FISH SERIES

PRAISE

THE BEST OF CONTEMPORARY ~~~~ MUSIC

ISBN 978-1-4234-5637-7

HAL•LEONARD CORPORATION

7777 W. BLUEMOUND RD. P.O. BOX 13819 MILWAUKEE, WI 53213

Visit Hal Leonard Online at
www.halleonard.com

AGNUS DEI

Words and Music by
MICHAEL W. SMITH

BE GLORIFIED

Words and Music by
BILLY FUNK

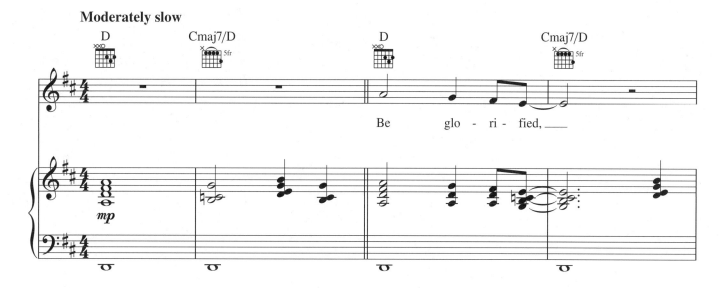

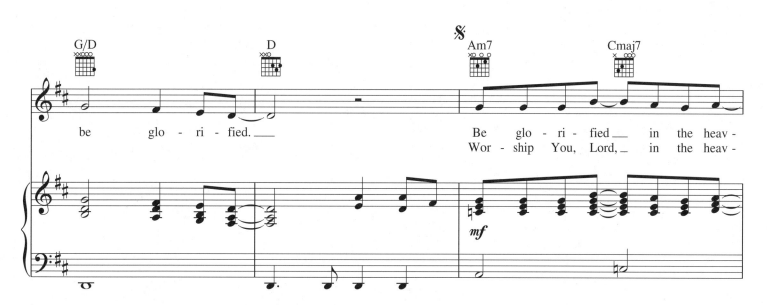

ALL HAIL KING JESUS

Words and Music by
DAVE MOODY

THE BATTLE BELONGS TO THE LORD

Words and Music by
JAMIE OWENS COLLINS

BECAUSE WE BELIEVE

Words and Music by NANCY GORDON
and JAMIE HARVILL

With praise

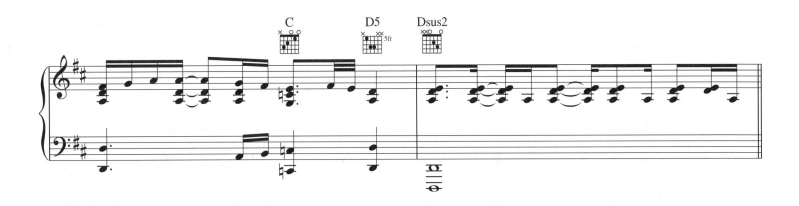

We be - lieve___ in God the Fa - ther,___
We be - lieve___ in the Ho - ly Bi - ble,___

glo-ry___ and hon-or___ are His to___ re-ceive. To

Je-sus___ we sing___ be-cause we___ be-lieve.

lieve.

And

D.S. al Coda

CODA

we are the Church _ and we stand as one.

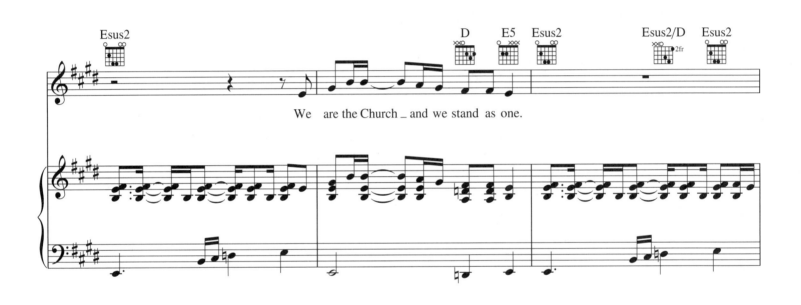

We are the Church _ and we stand as one.

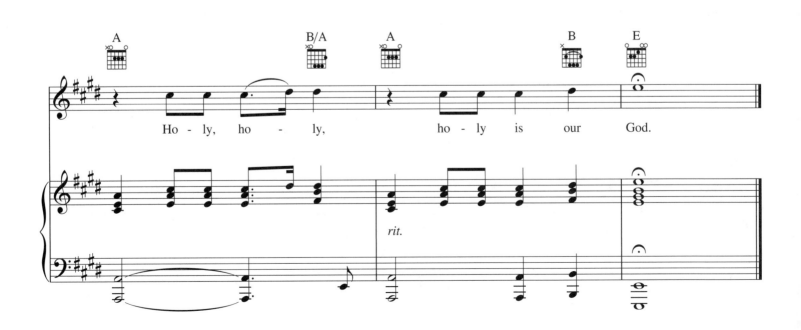

Ho - ly, ho - ly, ho - ly is our God.

rit.

BEFORE THE THRONE OF GOD ABOVE

Words and Music by VIKKI COOK
and CHARITIE BANCROFT

With reverence

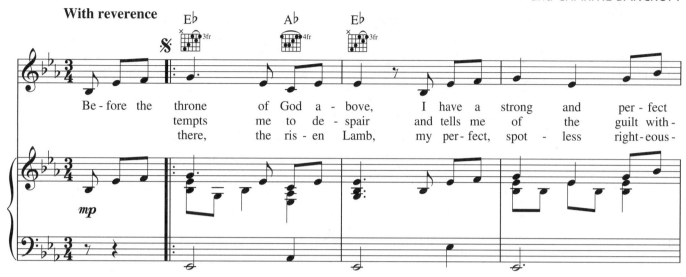

Be-fore the throne of God a-bove, I have a strong and per-fect
tempts me to de-spair and tells me of the guilt with-
there, the ris-en Lamb, my per-fect, spot-less right-eous-

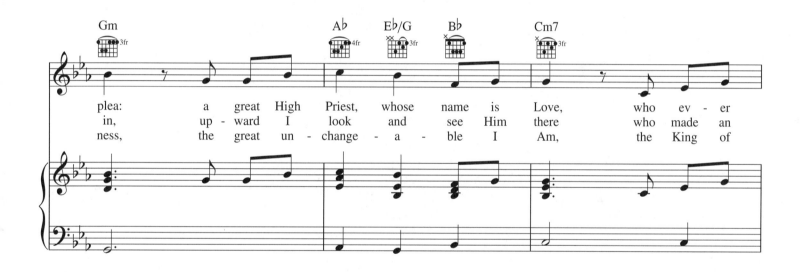

plea: a great High Priest, whose name is Love, who ev-er
in, up-ward I look and see Him there who made an
ness, the great un-change-a-ble I Am, the King of

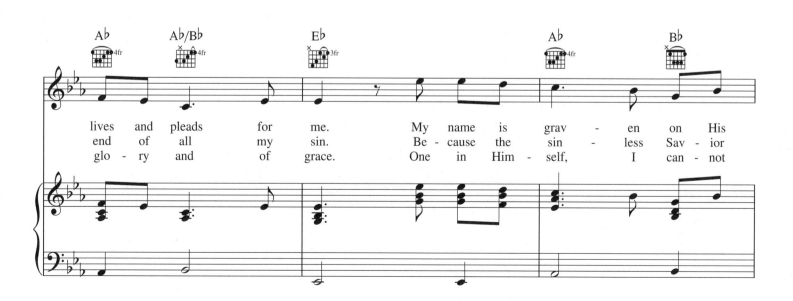

lives and pleads for me. My name is grav-en on His
end of all my sin. Be-cause the sin-less Sav-ior
glo-ry and of grace. One in Him-self, I can-not

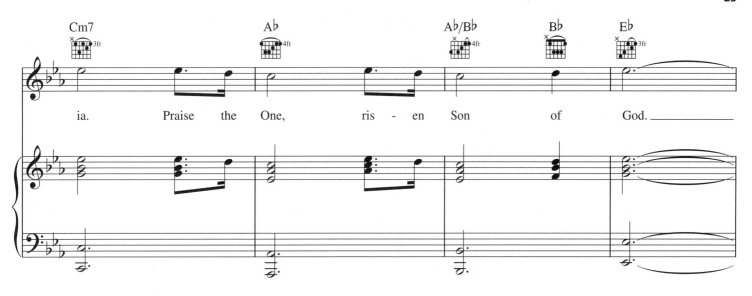

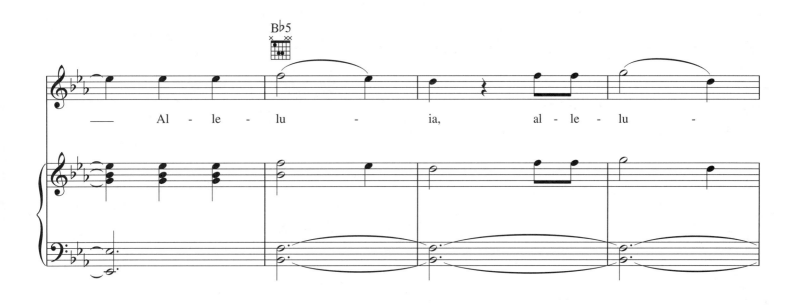

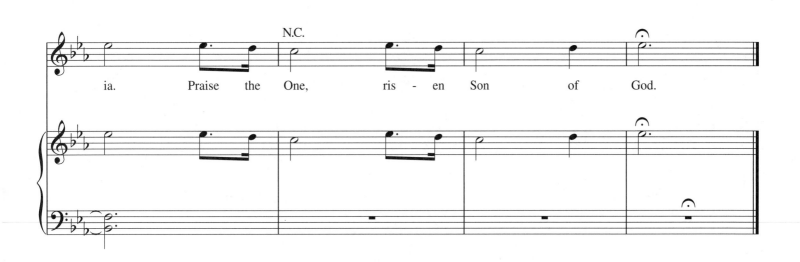

BIND US TOGETHER

Words and Music by
BOB GILLMAN

BLESSED BE THE NAME
OF THE LORD

Words and Music by
DON MOEN

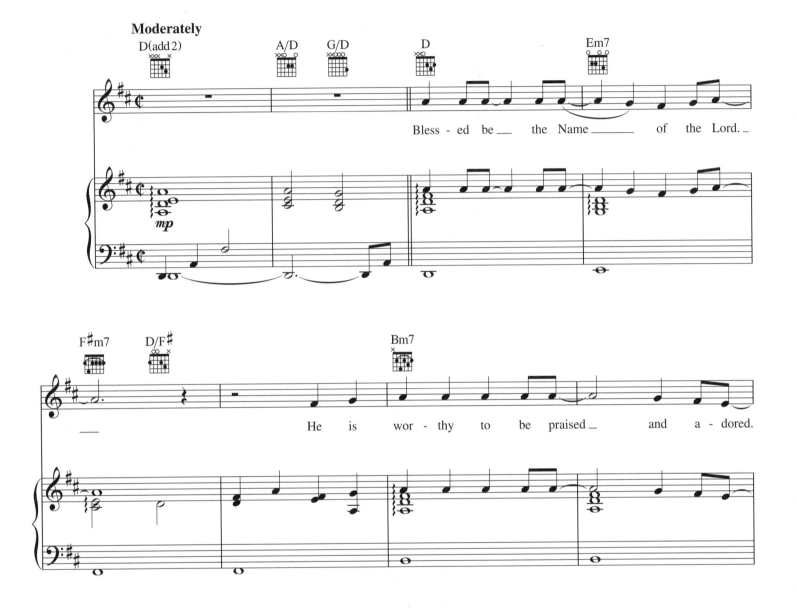

Moderately

Bless-ed be __ the Name __ of the Lord. __

He is wor-thy to be praised __ and a-dored.

So, we lift up ho-ly hands __ in one ac-cord,

CELEBRATE THE LORD OF LOVE

Words and Music by PAUL BALOCHE
and ED KERR

COME INTO HIS PRESENCE

Words and Music by
LYNN BAIRD

Come in-to ___ His pres-ence with thanks-giv-ing in ___ your heart and give Him praise, and give Him praise.

Come in-to ___ His pres-ence with thanks-giv-ing in ___ your heart, your voic-es

COME JUST AS YOU ARE

Words and Music by
JOE SABOLICK

Come just as you are,

hear the Spir - it call. Come just as you

are.

Come and see, come re - ceive,
Come re - ceive Christ the King,

GOD IS GOOD ALL THE TIME

Words and Music by DON MOEN
and PAUL OVERSTREET

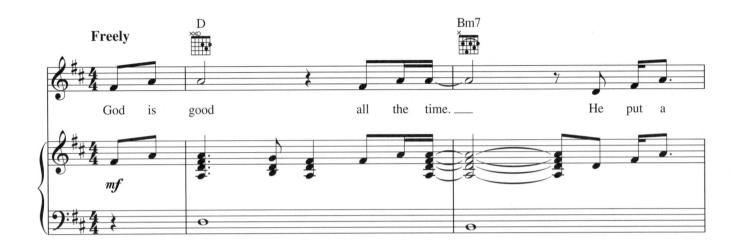

God is good all the time. __ He put a

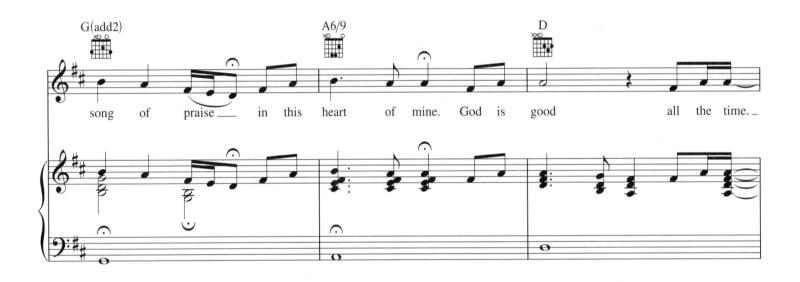

song of praise __ in this heart of mine. God is good all the time. __

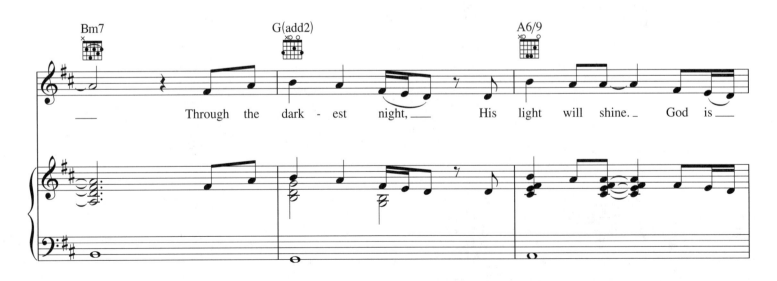

Through the dark-est night, __ His light will shine. __ God is __

time.

HE KNOWS MY NAME

Words and Music by
TOMMY WALKER

I have __ a Ma - ker; __
I have __ a Fa - ther; __
Instrumental

He formed ____ me my heart. ____
He calls ____ me His own. ____

Be - fore ____ e - ven time be - gan, ____ my
He'll nev - er ____ leave ____ me, ____ no

I LOVE TO BE IN YOUR PRESENCE

Words and Music by PAUL BALOCHE
and ED KERR

Lyrics:

I love to be ___ in Your pres - ence, with Your peo - ple ___ sing - ing prais - es; I love to stand ___ and re - joice, ___

HOLY AND ANOINTED ONE

Words and Music by
JOHN BARNETT

HOLY GROUND

Words and Music by
GERON DAVIS

I OFFER MY LIFE

Words and Music by DON MOEN
and CLAIRE CLONINGER

Lord, I of-fer my life ___ to You. Ev-'ry-thing I've ___ been through, ___

I WILL CALL UPON THE LORD

Words and Music by
MICHAEL O'SHIELDS

64

I'M FOREVER GRATEFUL

Words and Music by
MARK ALTROGGE

IN THE PRESENCE

Words and Music by
MARK ALTROGGE

JESUS IS ALIVE

Words and Music by
RON KENOLY

THE JOY OF THE LORD

Words and Music by
TWILA PARIS

The joy of ___ the Lord
joy of ___ the Lord

will be ___ my strength.	I will ___ not fal - ter,	I will ___ not ___ faint.
will be ___ my strength.	He will ___ up-hold me	all of ___ my ___ days.

LET IT RISE

Words and Music by
HOLLAND DAVIS

(1.,3.) glo - ry of __ the Lord __ rise a - mong __ us. Let the
(2.) songs __ of __ the Lord __ rise a - mong __ us. Let the

JESUS, WHAT A BEAUTIFUL NAME

Words and Music by
TANYA RICHES

Flowing

Je - sus, what a beau - ti - ful name;

Son of God, Son of Man, Lamb that was slain.

Joy and peace, strength and hope, grace that blows all

For-give-ness, se - cu - ri - ty, pow - er and love,
Joy and peace, strength and love, hope,

grace that blows all fear a - way. ____ Je - sus,

what a beau - ti - ful name.

name.   Joy and peace, strength and

LET THERE BE GLORY AND HONOR AND PRAISES

Words and Music by
ELIZABETH GREENELSH

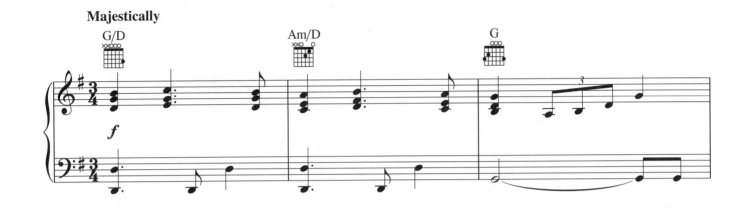

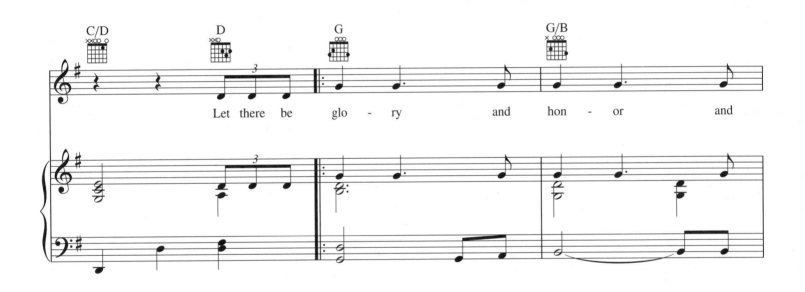

LOVE YOU SO MUCH

Words and Music by
RUSSELL FRAGAR

With praise

Hear these prais-es from a grate-ful heart. ___ Each time I think of You the prais-es start. ___ Love You so much, ___ Je - sus, ___ love You

MAJESTY

Words and Music by
JACK W. HAYFORD

MOURNING INTO DANCING

Words and Music by
TOMMY WALKER

With rhythmic energy

NO OTHER NAME

Words and Music by
ROBERT GAY

D.S. al Coda
(with repeat)

NOW UNTO HIM

Words by DAVID W. MORRIS, Based on Jude 24-25
Music by DAVID W. MORRIS

OH HOW HE LOVES YOU AND ME

Words and Music by
KURT KAISER

ONE PURE AND HOLY PASSION

Words and Music by
MARK ALTROGGE

ONLY BY GRACE

Words and Music by
GERRIT GUSTAFSON

Only by grace can we en-ter, only by grace can we stand.

OPEN OUR EYES

Words and Music by
BOB CULL

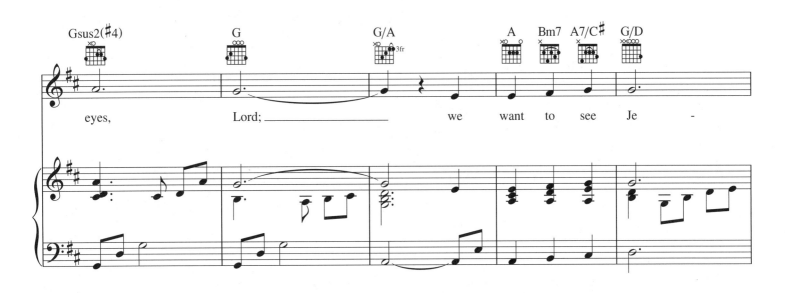

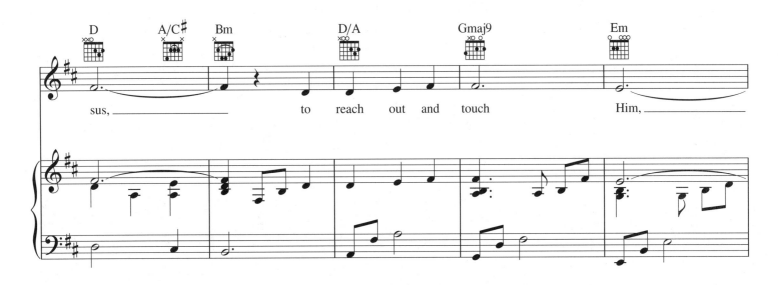

OUR GOD REIGNS

Words and Music by
LEONARD SMITH

THE POWER OF YOUR LOVE

Words and Music by
GEOFF BULLOCK

Lord, I come to You. ___ Let my heart ___ be changed, re- newed, ___
Lord, un- veil my eyes. ___ Let me see ___ You face to ___ face, ___

flow- ing from the grace ___ that I found ___
the knowl- edge of Your love ___ as You live ___

*Recorded a half step lower.

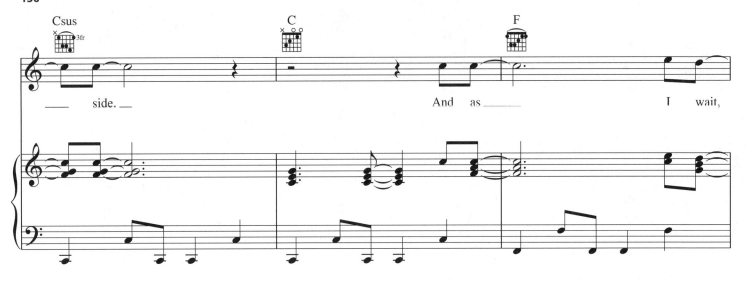

side. And as I wait,

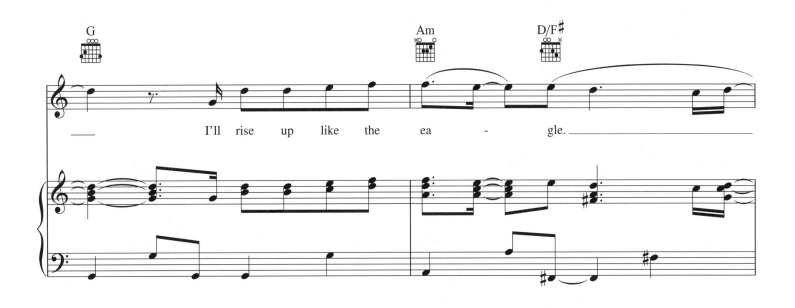

I'll rise up like the ea - gle.

And I will soar with You, Your Spir - it leads me on

by the pow'r of Your love.

Your Spir - it leads me on by the pow'r of Your love.

Your Spir - it leads me.

PRAISE THE NAME OF JESUS

Words and Music by
ROY HICKS, JR.

Stately Hymn

Praise the name of Je - sus! Praise the name of Je -

RISE UP AND PRAISE HIM

Words and Music by PAUL BALOCHE
and GARY SADLER

SHOW ME YOUR WAYS

Words and Music by
RUSSELL FRAGAR

SING FOR JOY

Words and Music by
LAMONT HIEBERT

THAT'S WHY WE PRAISE HIM

Words and Music by
TOMMY WALKER

THERE IS JOY IN THE LORD

Words and Music by
CHERI KEAGGY

THOU ART WORTHY

Words and Music by
PAULINE MICHAEL MILLS

WONDERFUL, MERCIFUL SAVIOR

Words and Music by DAWN RODGERS
and ERIC WYSE

for, oh, _____ our _____ hearts al - ways

hun - ger for. _____
(Vocal 1st time only)

Repeat and Fade

Optional Ending
Dsus2

TO HIM WHO SITS ON THE THRONE

Words and Music by
DEBBYE C. GRAAFSMA

WE HAVE COME INTO HIS HOUSE

Words and Music by
BRUCE BALLINGER

Lyrics:

We have come in-to His house and gath-ered in His name to
get a-bout our-selves and mag-ni-fy the Lord and

wor - ship Him. _____
wor - ship Him. _____

We have come in-to His house and
Let's for - get a - bout our-selves and

8vb

WORTHY OF WORSHIP

Words by TERRY YORK
Music by MARK BLANKENSHIP

WORTHY THE LAMB
THAT WAS SLAIN

Words and Music by
DON MOEN

Moderately

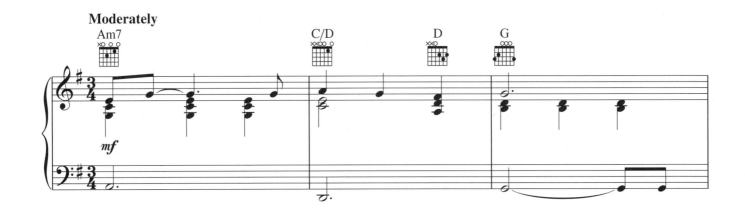

Wor - thy ___ the Lamb that was ___ slain,

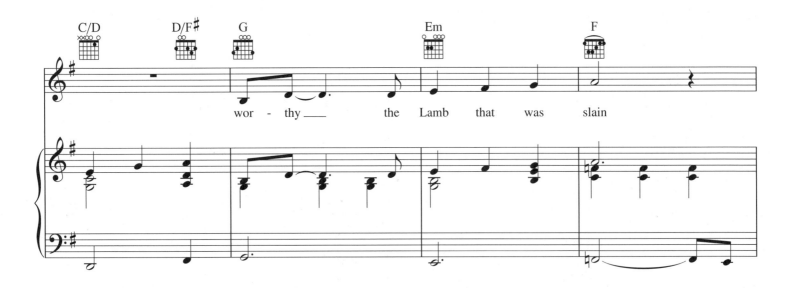

wor - thy ___ the Lamb that was slain

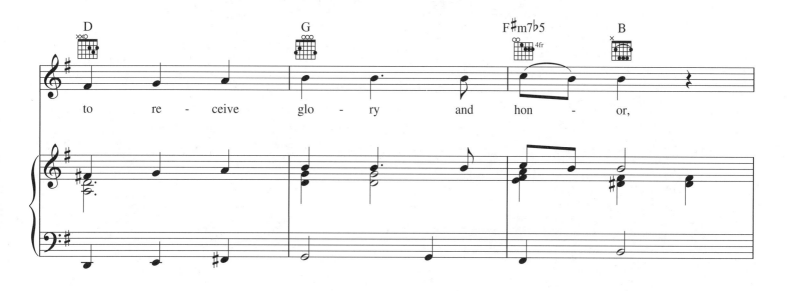

to re - ceive glo - ry and hon - or,

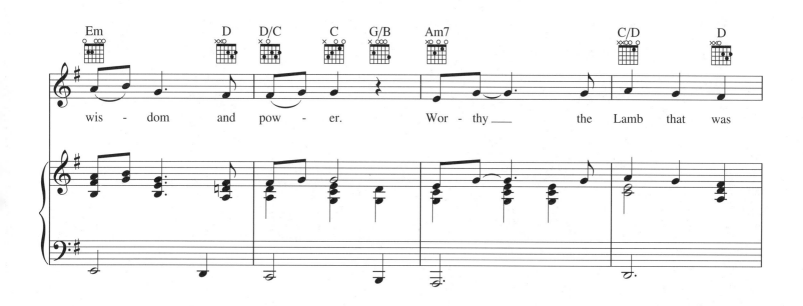

wis - dom and pow - er. Wor - thy ___ the Lamb that was

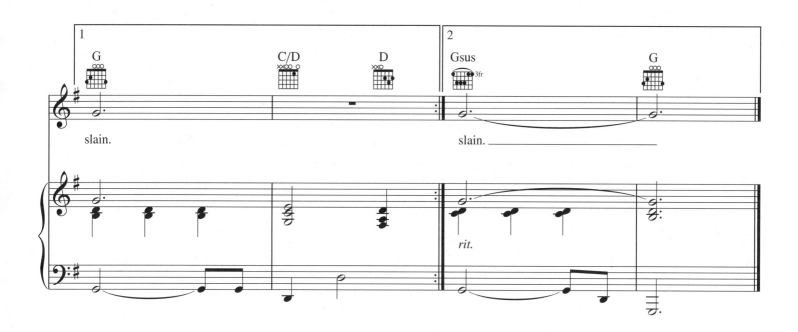

slain.

slain. _____

YOU ARE THE ONE

Words and Music by KEITH GREEN
and MELODY GREEN

YOU ARE MY ALL IN ALL

By DENNIS JERNIGAN